Sex Bible—Lectures from Female Experts

A document for sex was written in period between 770-221 BC and is still in wide use

Translator Jirong Liu

Sex Bible

Jirong Liu

Published by Great Wall Publishing, 2023.

SEX BIBLE

First edition. September 20, 2023.

Written by Jirong Liu.

Also Translated by Jirong Liu:

1. Simple wappiness in Sharingrity
2. A Story of Consort WateryJade Li
3. Blue Rattlesnake
4. Above Clouds
5. Under Sunshine
6. Black or White Ways

Contents

Part I Principles

Principle 1

Yellow Emperor asked:" I feel lack of energy and enthusiasm for doing things, worry about my body, think something dangerous might happen in any moment, what's wrong with my body?"

Pure Woman said:" The thing happens due to the imbalance of your body and inappropriateness of your sexual life. If the woman has a strong desire which could not be satisfied by a man, it just likes pouring water into a fire, which will dampen or inhibit the man's desire and make the man feel bad about himself. Sex between man and woman is just like cooking, the water and the fire must be balanced to get delicious food. If one can figure out the balance between the fire and the water and the cooperation between man and woman in sex, then one could benefit from the joy and happiness one could get from sex. Otherwise, one's body will be hurt in the process, which will damage one's body and shorten one's life, then how one could enjoy the most enjoyable thing in the world? How could one take sex casually and carelessly?"

PRINCIPLE 2

Pure Woman said:" There is a woman named Virtuoso Woman who knows sex very well."

Yellow Emperor sent Virtuoso Woman to ask more about how to have an enjoyable longevity from Ancestor Peng(* It was said he lived for eight hundred years, based on current knowledge about the length of time at that time he lived around eighty to ninety years old at current time scale).

Ancestor Peng said:" Cherish your body, cultivate your mind, take various supplements, then you will have a longevity. But if you don't understand how to have sex, then no matter how many supplements you will take, they will not bright about benefits to your longevity. The combination of man and woman is like the cooperation between the heaven and the earth which assist and balance each other, thus leads their perpetual existence without end. If one couldn't get to know how to have sex, then the sex will damage one's body and shorten one's life. If one understands how to have sex without hurting one's body and gets to know to adjust the balance between man and woman, then one will have and enjoy a happy longevity."

Virtuoso Woman bowed twice, said:"Could you please give me further explanation?"

Ancestor Peng said:" The reason behind the thing is very simple and easy to understand. Only the ordinary people either are lack of confidence or could not persist or practise it fully. At the moment Yellow Emperor has so many things to take care of which makes his body tired and his mind occupied, thus he definitely has no time to think about and understand various principles and methods for longevity. The lucky thing is that he has a wife and many concubines, so long as he understands the principles about how to have a healthy sex, thus he will definitely prolong his healthy life. The principle is to have sex with his wife and concubines as often as he could with fewer ejaculations as possible as he could, thus he will feel his spry body without any illness."

Principle 3

Pure Woman told Yellow Emperor:" When you have sex with a woman, you should take the woman as a cheap earthen brick and your body as an expensive jade. When you find the woman is about to reach climax through her body's rocking back and forth, you should immediately withdraw your penis out of her vagina. If you want to conquer a woman by sex, you have to be extremely careful when you have sex, just like you are riding a galloping horse with a rotten rein, or walking along an abyss covered with piercing knives at its bottom. If you cherish your semen and often could withhold your ejaculation, then you will be full of vitality, thus have an enjoyable longevity."

PRINCIPLE 4

Yellow Emperor asked:"I want to stop having sex for some time, in that case what will happen?"

Pure Woman said:" You cannot do in that way. In nature the sun will rise and set down every day, the earth will have day and night, each year there will be spring, summer, autumn and winter, everything will change according to certain time sequence. Man should also follow this kind of natural sequence. If you stop having sex, then your semen could not get out of your body, your mind will not be soothed by sexual activity, your body will lose its balance. Then how could your body assimilate and supplement itself? You have to keep practising breathing adjustment technique to exhale waste gas and inhale fresh air to promote your health. If your penis does not often insert into vagina to have sex, it will lose its function just like a snake coils and immobilizes in its den, therefore, you have to learn to practise the breathing adjustment technique to promote the vitality distribution in your body, thus to keep your vitality and energy moving and circulating smoothly in your body. When you have sex, you should practise the technique of rejuvenation of your semen, thus you will not waste your semen, you could save the vital part of your semen in your body, therefore you could have full vitality in your spirit and strength."

PRINCIPLE 5

Yellow Emperor asked:" How could one decide the frequency of sex?'" Pure Woman said:" It's a human nature to have sex. The frequency should be taken as appropriate so long as man doesn't feel lack of energy and weakened body, woman doesn't incur any illness, and the couple have a happy and enjoyable life and strong bodies full of vitality. If one doesn't know how to have sex, then one's body will be weakened and one will feel lack of vitality. In fact the essence for having sex is to have a peaceful mind, relaxed body with vitality and energy. If one could have the status with a peaceful and relaxed mind, then one will definitely not be afraid of coldness, hotness, hunger or overfeeding, thus one could have best body status with relaxed mind and mood for sex. When one has sex, one still has to follow the principle for shallow penetration and slow movement. The essence is to let the woman have pleasure and the man keep his vitality and energy without weakening his body."

PRINCIPLE 6

Yellow Emperor asked:"I have acquired some knowledge and outlines about how to have sex from Pure Woman, could you please give me further explanation?" Profound Woman said:"Every living thing in the world originates from the copulation of opposite sexes. The male will be nurtured by the female, the female will be protected by the male, they help and assist each other, respond to each other to prolong life. Therefore, as soon as man's penis touches the vagina, it will enlarge and erect; as soon as the female is stimulated, her vagina will open to accept the penis, thus the male and female could copulate, the secretions will be exchanged, the resonance and joy will be followed. During copulation, man has to follow eight precepts and woman nine commandments. If they don't follow these precepts and commandments to have inappropriate sex, the man will catch ulcer and abscess, the woman will have irregular period and various diseases, in the end they will lose lives and part the world forever. In contrast, if they could follow these precepts and commandments to have appropriate sex, they will have a healthy and happy longevity."

Part II Psychology and physiology

Principle 1

Yellow Emperor asked:" What a kind of principle one has to follow when one has copulation?" Pure Woman said:" Copulation is an inborn nature depending on species and a natural phenomenon. Through copulation man will have a strong body full of vitality and woman will be free of illnesses, the couple will have happy feeling with healthy bodies. If one doesn't know how to have copulation, then one's body will be damaged and weakened in the process. Then what is the principle of copulation? That is for copulation one has to have a peaceful mind, relaxed body, quiet mood, and healthy body with a happy feeling. Based on this principle, one has to follow the practices for healthy longevity, one does not let one's body suffer extreme coldness and hotness, hunger and overfeeding. One has to have a bright mind, decent and upright behavior, thus one could get peaceful mind and happy feeling. At the beginning of copulation, one has to have shallow and slow penetration and movement, make fewer back and forth movements, this is the essence for copulation, which should not be violated. By following the principle, woman will get pleasure from the copulation and man will get a healthy body filled with vitality."

PRINCIPLE 2

Yellow Emperor asked:" I wanted to have copulation but my penis is impotent, I felt totally ashamed in front of my woman, my body was covered with sweats, I did not know where I should hide myself. Even if I forced my penis into her vagina, it still did not work. For such a kind of thing, how could I become potent again? Please tell me the secret recipes in detail to cope with the impotence!" Pure Woman said:" Your question is very common among men. If a man wants to have copulation with a woman, the man has to prepare psychologically according to certain sequence. First, the man has to have a peaceful mind, only through a peaceful mind the penis will become erected naturally. If the man follows a natural way according to certain sequence, the woman will definitely show nine responses. Woman will show five phenomenon in her sexual desire, when the phenomena are fully developed, her body will be filled with vitality and energy. At the moment the man could suck back and swallow her saliva to get the vitality and energy back into his body and fill his brain, thus he could avoid to violate the seven precepts, naturally follow the eight beneficial ways without paying particular attention to the copulation. Then he will maintain his healthy body full with vitality and energy, in such a way he will no longer worry about his body. If his organs function normally, then he will show lustre in his face and vitality in his body. For each copulation he will have his erected penis as hard as iron with full power, it is so easy for him to get woman into her climax, thus he will never be ashamed with sweats covered body again from impotence."

Principle 3

Yellow Emperor asked:" When a man has copulation, the woman does not get any pleasure without any arousal and vaginal lubrication and secretion. The man's penis is impotent and soft and powerless, what's the cause?" Profound Woman said:" Copulation has to be accomplished by a couple through mutual stimulation and response. Thus the woman could only get pleasure from stimulation of the man, in same reason, the man could only erect from the stimulation of the woman. If the woman does not get sufficient stimulation from the man, the man wants to insert his penis into her vagina, the woman definitely could not get pleasure from the act. In the same reason, if the woman wants to have copulation and the man does not get sufficient stimulation, the man definitely could not erect. If the couple don't have the feeling and desire at the same time, one definitely could not arouse the desire of the other for copulation, under such a kind of circumstance, if one forces the other to have copulation, the one has to act roughly and rudely, thus naturally it will lead to disgust of the other. In contrast, if the man wants to have copulation, and the woman has same desire too, they will act synchronously, the woman will have a strong desire with charming expression and touching moaning, thus the man will erect at once with full energy, some secretion will come out of his balanus, at this time the man should put some pressure on the lower abdomen of the woman, then insert his penis into the vagina, the man could make back and forth movements easily according to his own desire. The vagina of the woman will constrict and relax accordingly. Thus the man could make the woman get much pleasure without spending much energy. At the moment the man should suck her saliva and absorb the vitality and energy of the woman to supplement his own energy. Eight skills of copulation include stretch and bend, bend forward and backward, thrush forward and withdraw backward, turn and twist around, I hope you will get to know the skills and utilize them skillfully."

PRINCIPLE 4

Yellow Emperor asked:"For the copulation, does one have to follow certain sequence?" Pure Woman said:" Before the man does the copulation with a woman, first he has to let the woman lie down peacefully and calmly, bend and open her legs. Then the man prostrates between her legs, kisses her lips, sucks her tongue, uses his own hand to hold his penis to tease her vagina and its around area for a while, then slowly insert his penis into the vagina. For the man with big penis, he can insert for about three and half centimeters, for the man with small penis, he can insert for about two and half centimeters, at the beginning, he cannot rock from side to side, he should just withdraw his penis slowly from the vagina, and repeat the process. The method could cure many illness. When the man has the ejaculation, he should not let his semen come out of the vagina. When the man inserts his penis into the vagina, his penis will be stimulated by the process and ejaculation is a natural consequence of the process. At the time the woman would rock her body back and forth to cooperate with the man subconsciously and spontaneously. At the moment, the man could insert his penis deeply into the vagina, naturally the process will cure all their diseases. Then the man could withdraw his penis and stimulate the clitoris with his penis, then inserts deep for about eight centimeters, the vagina will contract around the penis, then the man begins to count from one to nine, the man inserts his penis deeper further into the vagina, during the insertion and withdrawal process, the man should kiss and suck her lips, repeat the process for many times as one could. This is the sequence for copulation."

PRINCIPLE 5

Yellow Emperor asked:" What are the five cardinal virtues?" Pure Woman said:" The penis has to follow five rules. In normal time it has to hide and act itself well like an eremite, protect itself like a recluse who practices abstinence with grand benevolence. If it wants to act on someone, it should act benevolently without saving its effort, this should be called benevolence; it has a duct in the middle, which should be taken as justice; it has a balanus, which should be taken as propriety; it could erect when it wants to copulate and it would retract to its normal status when it does not want to have copulation, which should be taken as honour; when it does the copulation, it will do the copulation peacefully, carefully and thoughtfully, which should be taken as wisdom. Therefore gentleman usually follow the five cardinal virtues to control his own desire for copulation. Though a man wants to do copulation with a woman by following benevolence, he could not erect due to lack of energy, then he has to do abstinence and tell the woman frankly, thus to avoid damage to his body due to excessive copulation, this is the principle of abstinence. If the status of one's body allows to do copulation, one has to do the copulation with propriety and honour. Such kind of practices will also demonstrate the man really knows how to do copulation. Therefore, if one could follow and practice the five cardinal virtues, then one could have a happy and enjoyable longevity.

PRINCIPLE 6

Yellow Emperor asked:"How could one get to know the woman is having pleasures?" Pure Woman said:" There are five signs, five desires and ten movements to observe. If one sees the phenomena, then one will know the woman gets the pleasure from the copulation. For five signs: When the face of the woman turns pinkish or reddish, the man could put his penis lightly at the mons pubis; when the nipples harden and there is slight perspiration around the nose, the man could insert his penis slowly into the vagina; when the woman shows dry lips and swallows her saliva, the man could slowly rock his penis from side to side in the vagina; when the vagina has secretions and lubrication, the man could insert his penis deeply and slowly further into the vagina; when there are a lot of secretions flowing out of the vagina down into the buttock, the man could slowly withdraw his penis from the vagina"

Pure Woman said:" From five desires, the man could get to know the responses of the woman. First is that when the woman wants to be embraced tightly, she would hold breath to wait to be embraced; second is that when the woman wants her private parts to be caressed, her nostrils and mouth would open and close alternately; third is that when the desire of the woman is greatly aroused, she would rock her body back and forth and from side to side and embrace the man tightly; fourth is that when the woman reaches her climax and her desire is completely satisfied, her body would be covered with sweats and her clothes are drenched with sweats; fifth is that if the woman gets extreme pleasure, she would feel her body floating and her soul leaving like in fairyland without her own realization."

Pure Woman said: " For the ten movements of the woman which show her pleasure: First, when the woman embraces the man, she wants to hold the man tightly to make tight contact of their private parts; second, the woman would stretch her legs forwardly and upwardly, thus to get more rubbing above upper part of her vagina; third the woman would expose her abdomen to ingratiate the man, thus she wants the man to insert into her vagina; fourth, the woman would rock her buttocks back and forth and from side to side, which demonstrates the woman has already had the pleasure; fifth the woman bends her feet to hold the man's body, which means she wants the man inserts his penis further into her vagina; sixth the woman's two thighs cross together, which means the woman could hardly control her own sexual lust; seventh the woman's waist moves sideways, which means the she wants the penis moves further and rocks from side to side; eighth the woman bends her body upward and attaches to the man tightly, which means she will come to climax in any moment; ninth the woman's whole body stretch completely while rocking back and forth, which means she comes to the complete and happy climax; tenth a lot of secretions come out of vagina, which means she has finished her climax. Based on the above ten movements, one could judge the extent of pleasure of the woman."

PRINCIPLE 7

Yellow Emperor asked:"One wants to keep on copulation but one's penis is soft, could one force oneself to continue?" Profound Woman said:"No! Only when man has four ready statuses, then the man could do copulation. Only when woman has nine thorough functions, then the woman could do copulation."

Yellow Emperor asked:" What are the four ready statuses?" Profound Woman said:" His penis is not erect, that means he lacks of sufficient stored energy; his penis is erect without hardness, that means he lacks of muscle strength; his penis is hard without firmness, that means he lacks of tendon strength; his penis is firm without hotness, that means he lacks of internal strength. Therefore if the penis is erect, that means it has enough stored energy with fighting spirit; if the penis is hard, that means it has sufficient power to attack; if the penis is firm, that means it is ready to shoot; if the penis is hot, that means a pot is on the strong flame, and none could stop the boiling water within the pot, the man is ready for copulation. Even if one has the stored energy, muscle strength, tendon strength and internal strength with good fighting spirit, one still has to get to know and practice abstinence to save one's inborn strength. One could not copulate as one likes, even if one copulates, one should not ejaculate indiscriminately."

Yellow Emperor said:"You are right! What are the nine thorough functions of the woman?"

Profound Woman said:" It is not difficult to observe the nine thorough functions of the woman. With rapid breath and swallow of saliva, it means the lung functions thoroughly; with the continuous moaning and kissing the man, it means the heart functions thoroughly; with embracing with two arms and twisting around the man, it means the spleen functions thoroughly; with slippery wetness in private parts and misty eyes, it means the kidney functions thoroughly; with bending feet and wrapping around the thighs of the man, it means the tendon functions thoroughly; with tender fingers to caress penis, it means the blood functions thoroughly; with confused mind and caressing the nipples of the man, it means the muscle functions thoroughly. When a man has a copulation with a woman, the man has to caress her body and observe carefully for her nine functions, he has to wait for right time to get copulation naturally and smoothly and effortlessly, otherwise their bodies will be harmed. If the man notices deficiency in one of the functions, he can correct the deficiency through appropriate skills of copulation."

Part III Postures

Method 1 Dragon Plough

Yellow Emperor asked:" You mentioned nine postures for copulation, please explain each method in details, thus the methods could be recorded as a booklet, and could be preserved and practised." Profound Woman said:" First is called Dragon Plough: the woman lies in supine position, the man climbs over the woman, the thighs of the man are between the legs of the woman. The private parts of the woman greets the penis, the man uses his penis to stimulate the clitoris and the upper part of the private parts, then inserts and thrushes into the vagina slowly, inserts shallowly for eight times, then inserts deeply twice. When the penis hardens, the man withdraws his penis from the vagina, waits his penis to soften a bit, then repeats the process and follows the principle to withdraw when it hardens and to insert when it softens. By following the practice, the penis will become stronger and stronger, the woman will get extremely happy and joyful pleasures with charming expressions, the vagina of the woman will contract tightly, which will help to cure various diseases."

Method 2 Tiger Crouch

Second is called Tiger Crouch: the woman prostrates her body, raises her buttocks, lowers her head, the man kneels down behind her buttocks, embraces her waist and abdomen, inserts his penis deeply into the vagina, pushes forth and pulls back rapidly for about forty times. The man can determines the times accordingly. When the vagina begins to contract and tighten, secretions come out of the vagina, the man withdraws his penis completely out of the vagina to have a complete rest. If the couple follow the method, they would maintain their healthy status and the man would become stronger and more powerful.

Method 3 Ape Fight

Third is called Ape Fight: the woman lies in supine position while raising her legs, the man kneels down behind the thighs while facing the woman, uses his hands to support her legs and put her legs onto his shoulders to make her knees above the level of the chest and lift up the back of her buttocks a bit, then inserts his penis and stimulates the upper part of her vagina, the woman will get maximal pleasure and secretions from her vagina will drop down like raindrops. The man inserts his penis further into her vagina, then the penis will harden further, after the woman reaches her climax, then the copulation will be done. If the couple follow the method, they will be free of any illnesses.

Method 4 Cicada Attach

Fourth is called Cicada Attach: the woman prostrates her body completely, the man climbs on her back, inserts his penis deeply into her vagina, the woman raises her legs a bit, the man thrashes his penis back and forth for fifty four times, after the woman gets completely stimulated with a lot of secretions, the vagina shivers and contracts due to the thrash, and the woman reaches her climax, then the man stops his thrashing. If the couple follows the method, it will cure the illnesses related to anger, anxiety, worry, sadness, terror, fright and overjoy.

Method 5 Tortoise Mount

The fifth is called Tortoise Mount: Let the woman lie in supine position while bending her knees to her chest, the man kneels in front of the woman while facing her, uses his hands to push her lower legs to her breasts, inserts his penis deeply into her vagina, then pushes forward and pulls back of his penis while stimulating her clitoris. For the back and forth movement, the depth of the penetration should be appropriate while paying attention to stimulate her clitoris in the process. By the method the woman will get pleasure very rapidly, and will naturally rock her body from side to side, a lot of secretions will come out of her vagina, then the man could insert his penis further down into her vagina, when the woman reaches her climax, the man stops his back and forth movement. If the couple follow the method, the man will become more energetic and powerful.

Method 6 Phoenix Flight

The sixth is called Phoenix Flight: The woman lie in supine position while extending her legs and bending her feet, the man kneels down between her legs while prostrating and supporting his body by his arms on bed. The man inserts his penis into her vagina while stimulating her clitoris. When the hardened and hot penis inserts into the vagina, the woman rocks her body from side to side for twenty four times while making sure the close contact between their private parts, the vagina will open due to excitement, a lot of secretions will spring out from the vagina, after the woman reaches her climax, the man stops his action. If the couple follow the method, they will naturally be free of illness.

Method 7 Rabbit Suck

The seventh is called Rabbit Suck: The man lies in supine position while extending his legs, the woman sits on the top of the man while facing his feet and kneeling down at his sides. The man inserts his penis into her vagina while stimulating her clitoris and the front part of the vagina. The woman will be excited easily with happy and joyful expressions and her secretions will spring out from her vagina, when the woman reaches her climax, then they stop their copulation. If the couple follow the method, they will naturally be free of illness.

Method 8 Fish Scale

The eighth is called Fish Scale: The man lies in supine position while extending his legs, the woman sits on the top of the man between his lower legs and thighs while facing the man. The woman moves her buttocks slowly forward to let her vagina swallow and bite his penis. Just let the penis insert shallowly just like a baby is suckling the nipple. The man should not try to make any movement, the woman controls all the movements and actions of back and forth and from side to side, the action will last for quite a while. When the woman reaches her climax, the man withdraws his penis out of the vagina and ends the copulation. If the couple follow the method, they will naturally be free of illness.

Method 9 Crane Neck

The ninth is called Crane Neck: The man sits in the bed while extending his legs, the woman rides on his body while putting her legs at his sides and holding his neck with her hands. The man inserts his penis into her vagina while stimulating her minor labia and clitoris. The man holds her buttocks to help her moving and rocking up and down and back and forth. After some time, a lot of secretions will rain down from her vagina, when the woman reaches her climax, then they should end the copulation. If the couple follow the method, it will cure the illnesses related to anger, anxiety, worry, sadness, terror, fright and over joy.

Part IV Strengthen Eight Body Functions and Get Rid of Seven Dysfunctions

Chapter 1 Strengthen Eight Body Functions

Pure Woman said:" Copulation between a couple could either benefit or harm their health, if the copulation is not appropriate, it will harm their bodies and minds.

First is called Strengthen Inborn Vitality: The woman lies on her side while extending her legs and the upper leg could bend slightly, the man lies on his side while facing the woman, inserts and withdraws his penis into her vagina for eighteen times continually, then stops the copulation completely. If the couple follow the method, it will strengthen the man's inborn vitality and concentrate the man's semen, and cures the woman's excessive menstruation. If the couple follow the method twice a day for fifteen days, it will cure vaginal bleeding and oligospermia.

Second is called Relieve Anxiety: The woman lies in supine position with a high pillow under her head, extends and spreads her legs, the man kneels down between her legs while supporting his body by his knees and palms and putting his palms at the sides of her arms. The man inserts and withdraws his penis into her vagina for twenty seven times, then stops the copulation completely. If the couple follow the method, it will tranquilize them and improve the circulation of their vitality and blood, and cure the frigidity of the woman. To get desirable effect, the couple have to practise the method three times per day for twenty days.

Third is called Store Energy: The woman lies on her side while bending her legs to expose buttocks and thighs as possible as she could, the man lies on his side while facing her back. The man inserts and withdraws his penis for thirty six times, then stops the copulation completely. The method will tranquilize the man and cure the frigidity of the woman. To get desirable effect, the couple have to practise the method four times per day for twenty days. The couple should not let the man ejaculate in the process.

Fourth is called Strengthen Bone: The woman lies on her left side while bending her left knee to her chest and extending her right leg, the man climbs and prostrates on her body, the man inserts and withdraws his penis into her vagina while facing downward, thus the front part of his penis will stimulate the lateral part of her vagina for forty five times, then stops the copulation completely. The method will loosen the bone joints, enliven their bodies, and cure the amenorrhea of the woman. To get desirable effect, the couple have to practise the method five times per day for ten days.

Fifth is called Adjust Circulation: The woman lies on her right side while bending her right knee to her chest and extending her left leg, the man climbs and prostrates on her body, the man inserts and withdraws his penis into her vagina while facing downward, thus the front part of his penis will stimulate the lateral part of her vagina for fifty four times, then stops the copulation completely. The method could adjust their circulations and cure the vaginismus. To get desirable effect, the couple have to practise the method six times per day for twenty days.

The sixth is called Store Blood: The man lies in supine position, the woman straddles on his thighs whiling kneeling at his sides to let her vagina face his penis, the woman lets her vagina wrap his penis and let the penis insert deeply into and withdraw from her vagina for sixty three times, then stops the copulation completely. The method will strengthen the man's body and cure the irregular menses. To get desirable effect, the couple have to practise the method seven times per day for ten days.

The seventh is called Benefit Body Liquid: The woman prostrates on the bed while putting a high pillow under her abdomen and thighs to raise her buttocks to expose her vagina as possibly as she could to let the penis insert, the man supports his body with his palms and knees and puts his feet at the sides of her legs, inserts and withdraws his penis for seventy two times. The method will make their bones and muscles strong.

The eighth method is called Improve Passage: The woman lies in supine position, bends her feet backward, and let her heels touch her buttocks, the man supports his body with his palms and knees and puts his feet at her sides, inserts and withdraws his penis for eighty one times, then stops the copulation completely. The method could cure the foul odor of the vagina. To get desirable effect, the couple have to practise the method nine times per day for nine days.

Chapter 2 Get Rid of Seven Dysfunctions

The first method is to get rid of lack of sexual desire: Lack of sexual desire happens due to the exhaustion of inborn vitality. If one forces to do copulation with the other without sexual desire, the other will be covered with sweats without enthusiasm, though the other could get excited without being able to open eyes. To get rid of this kind of dysfunction: Let the woman lie in supine position, the man first raises her legs, then inserts his penis into her vagina, let her move her body till her vaginal secretions flow out, then stops the copulation completely. It is a principle to follow that the man should not ejaculate in the process. If the couple follow the method for nine times per day for ten days, the dysfunction will be cured.

The second method is to get rid of premature ejaculation: Premature ejaculation happens when one has a strong desire for copulation, but before the process could come to a natural end, the man ejaculates first, particularly for the drunkard if he has copulation he will gasp and have irregular breath and harm the function of his lung accompanied by coughing, thirst, dryness in his throat and obstruction of urination etc. To get rid of this kind of dysfunction: Let the woman lie in supine position while bending her knees and wrapping her legs around the man, the man inserts his penis into her vagina for about three and half centimeters, let the woman rock her waist from side to side till vaginal secretions flow out, then stops the copulation completely. It is a principle to follow that the man should not ejaculate in the process. If the couple follow the method for nine times per day for ten days, the dysfunction will be cured.

The third method is to get rid of partial impotence: Partial impotence happens when one could just only force to insert his penis into her vagina, the penis is not hard enough, thus before the process could come to a natural end, the man will ejaculate first which leads to further exhaustion of his inborn vitality. When one has copulation with his full stomach as soon as he finishes his food, it will harm the function of the spleen which will lead to dysfunction of digestion and partial impotence and loss of inborn vitality. To get rid of this kind of dysfunction: Let the woman lie in supine position while wrapping her legs around his buttocks, the man supports his body while putting his hands on the bed, then inserts his penis into her vagina, then let the woman rock her body. When the woman reaches climax, they should end the copulation completely. If the couple follow the method for nine times per day for ten days, the dysfunction will be cured though the man does not get pleasure in the process.

Fourth method is to get rid of weakness in waist and knees, dizziness and tinnitus and impotence as so-called leakage of vitality: The leakage of vitality happens dues to forced sex after physical exhaustion with body still covered with sweats which leads to hot feeling in abdomen and dryness in lips. To get rid of leakage of vitality: Let the man lie in supine position while extending his body fully, the woman straddles on his body while facing his feet, then the woman supports her body with her knees and lower legs while locking the penis with her vagina in shallow penetration, then rocks her waist till she reaches her climax, then stops the copulation completely. It is a principle to follow that the man should not ejaculate in the process. If the couple follow the method for nine times per day for ten days, the dysfunction will be cured.

Fifth method is to prevent further damage due to malfunctions of other parts of the body due to chronic illness: For the man with chronic illness, he has difficulty in urination and defecation, after the exhaustion of his strength through urination and defecation, before his strength recovers, he takes chance to do copulation, which will harm the function of the liver, even if he does not exert much efforts in the process, he still will get his liver harmed, thus leads to the weakness in bone and tendons and lack of lustre in his eyes and malfunction of his circulation. If one persists in such a fashion, in long run it will lead to paralysis concurrent with impotence.

Sixth method is to get rid of lack of ejaculation: Lack of ejaculation happens due to the excessive sexual desire and impulse of the woman, which leads to lack of abstinence of the man, and the exhaustion of his inborn vitality, though the man wants to ejaculate, nothing will come out of his penis. This leads to various illness including the dryness in throat, obstruction of urination, and dizziness. To get rid of lack of ejaculation: Let the man lie supine position, the woman straddles and prostrate her body while facing the man and supporting her body with her hands on the bed, then the woman lets her vagina lock the penis, then rocks her body, stops after she gets satisfaction. It is a principle to follow that the man should not ejaculate in the process. If the couple follow the method for nine times per day for ten days, the dysfunction will be cured.

Seventh method is to get rid of bloody semen: Bloody semen happens when the man is tired after hard work or fast walk with his body still covered with sweats, at the moment he has the copulation. After he reaches his climax, he does the copulation again for quite a long time, thus which leads to complete exhaustion of his inborn vitality and sudden illnesses such as continual flowing of secretions from the penis, the exhaustion of his blood, change of his skin color, pain in his urethra, wetness around his scrotum and blood in his semen. To get rid of this illness: Let the woman lie in supine position while putting something under her buttocks to raise her buttocks and extending her legs, the man kneels down between her legs, inserts his penis into her vagina, let the woman rock her body, as soon as she gets her satisfaction, they should end the copulation. It is a principle to follow that the man should not ejaculate in the process. If the couple follow the method for nine times per day for ten days, the dysfunction will be cured.

CHAPTER 3 NO EJACULATION
critical to the health of man

Profound Woman asked:"Man gets maximal pleasure from ejaculation, if one demands the man to hold his ejaculation, then where could the man get pleasure from copulation?" Ancestor Peng said:"As soon as a man ejaculates, his body will feel very tired, his ears will have tinnitus, his eyesight will blur, he will feel sleepy, his mouth is dry, his body lacks strength, though he gets a moment of pleasure, in the end he does not feel long term pleasure. If one could hold his ejaculation in the copulation, then one will feel his body is filled with energy, his ears does not have tinnitus, his eyesight will be clear, though on the surface he feels not only suppressed but also peaceful and quiet, through such practice it will enhance the mutual loving relationship, isn't this kind of feeling is much better than the tiredness and sleepiness after ejaculation?"

Chapter 4 The benefits of no ejaculation

Yellow Emperor asked:" Though one wants to ejaculate, so long as he inhibits a bit, then he will not ejaculate, what are benefits from no ejaculation, could you please explain in detail?"

Pure Woman said:" At the completion of first successful copulation, if one just suppresses a bit, thus one will not ejaculate, then the man will feel energetic; at the completion of second successful copulation, if one just suppresses a bit, thus one will not ejaculate, then the man will be able to hear and see clearly; at the completion of third successful copulation, if one just suppresses a bit, thus one will not ejaculate, then the man will be free of illnesses; at the completion of fourth successful copulation, if one just suppresses a bit, thus one will not ejaculate, then the man will have normal functions of his internal organs; at the completion of fifth successful copulation, if one just suppresses a bit, thus one will not ejaculate, then the man will have good circulation with blood filled in his blood vessels; at the completion of sixth successful copulation, if one just suppresses a bit, thus one will not ejaculate, then the man will have strong back and waist; at the completion of seventh successful copulation, if one just suppresses a bit, thus one will not ejaculate, then the man will have powerful buttocks and thighs; at the completion of eighth successful copulation, if one just suppresses a bit, thus one will not ejaculate, then the body of the man will have shiny and charming lustre; at the completion of ninth successful copulation, if one just suppresses a bit, thus one will not ejaculate, then the man will naturally have his healthy longevity; at the completion of tenth successful copulation, if one just suppresses a bit, thus one will not ejaculate, then the man will open a door to become an immortal."

CHAPTER 5 PRINCIPLES of ejaculation

Yellow Emperor asked:" If the gist of copulation for man is no ejaculation, then one has to keep good storage for his semen. Nevertheless, if one wants to have a child, then one has to ejaculate."

Pure Woman said:" There are differences in body and age among people. Everyone tries to get maximal pleasure, but if one gets his maximal pleasure, then he might damage his body in the process. Therefore for man over fifteen years old, if he has a strong body, he could ejaculate twice a day, and if he has a weak body, he could ejaculate once a day without harming his body. In same way for man over twenty with a strong body, he could ejaculate twice a day and once a day with a weak body; for man over thirty with a strong body, he could ejaculate once a day and once every two days with a weak body; for man over forty with a strong body, he could ejaculate once every three days and once every four days with a weak body; for man over fifty with a strong body, he could ejaculate once every five days and once every ten days with a weak body; for man over sixty with a strong body, he could ejaculate once every ten days and once every twenty days with a weak body; for man over seventy with a strong body, he could ejaculate once every thirty days and no more with a weak body."

The frequencies adopted by Pure Woman were:" For man over twenty he will have an ejaculation every four days; for man over thirty he will have an ejaculation every eight days; for man over forty he will have an ejaculation every sixteen days; for man over fifty he will have an ejaculation every twenty days; for man over sixty he will have no more ejaculation, if the man is really strong, he could have an ejaculation every thirty days. There are differences among people, for people with particular strong body, even if he does not try to suppress his ejaculation, it might still be okay. If a man does not have ejaculation for a long time, then it will harm his body. If a man is over sixty, he is impotent and could not have copulation for dozens days, and is filled with anxiety, it is much better for him to have no ejaculation."

CHAPTER 6 SIGNS FOR strong or weak body

Profound Woman asked:" How could one judge a man has a strong or weak body?"

Ancestor Peng said:" If a man has a strong body filled with inborn vitality, then his penis is very hot and his semen is very concentrated. When a man has following five signs, then means the man has a weakened body: first premature ejaculation means his mind is weakened; second the amount of his semen is little and his semen is thin, that means his carnal body is weakened; third if his semen has foul smell, that means his tendon is weakened; fourth if his ejaculation is powerless, that means his bone is weakened; fifth if he is impotent, that means his body is weakened. Generally these dysfunctions arise from hasty copulation and ejaculation from uneasy mood. The method to get rid of these dysfunctions is: so long as one has copulation, one should persist in no ejaculation, then in less than one hundred days these dysfunctions will be corrected."

CHAPTER 7 HOW TO PREPARE for conception

Yellow Emperor said:" One comes after the copulation of a couple. Therefore the conception starts from copulation, in order to have normal and healthy conception, one has to avoid nine ominous periods: A child coming from conception at noon will have an eccentric and unreasonable and rash temperament; a child coming from conception in midnight will have a high probability for deaf as at the moment the sky and the earth are completely obstructed and dark and gloomy; a child coming from conception during solar eclipse will have a high probability for depression and illness; a child coming from conception during thunderstorm will have a high probability for madness as at the moment the sky is infuriating; a child coming from conception during lunar eclipse will have a high probability for difficult labor along with the suffering mother; a child coming from conception when huge natural disasters happen will have a high probability for bad outcome; a child coming from conception at the winter solstice day or summer solstice day will make the parents suffer; a child coming from conception at the full moon will have a high probability for suffering the turmoil of war; a child coming from conception when the parents are drunk will have a high probability for deforms, weak body, seizure, abscess, or ulcer."

CHAPTER 8 HOW TO GET best conception

Pure Woman said: "To get best conception a couple have to follow certain rules, the couple have to keep their bodies healthy with peaceful mood without worry and anxiety and neat clothes to have fast. After three days at the completion of the woman's period, in the period after midnight and before crowing, the couple should begin to caress. First let the woman get excited gradually, then the couple could do copulation by following the principles mentioned for the couple to enjoy the sexual pleasure together. When the man does his ejaculation, he should be careful not to withdraw his penis out of her vagina. Otherwise his semen could not enter the uterus. If the couple follows these rules, a child coming from such a kind of conception will be extraordinary and have longevity."

Pure Woman added:" The couple have to follow the rules mentioned to get best conception and avoid the ominous periods for conception. If the couple could have a conception at their best body conditions, then the child will have a high probability for longevity. If the couple are at old ages, even they have a conception at their best body conditions, the child usually will not have longevity."

CHAPTER 9 WHAT KIND of features could be taken as for a good woman

Yellow Emperor asked:" For a woman everyone likes, what kind of features should she have?"

Pure Woman said:" For a woman everyone likes, the woman should have a mild temperament, her voice is not hoarse and dry, her hairs should be thin and black, her muscle is lithe and flexible, her bone is delicate, her stature is neither tall nor short, she is neither fat nor thin, her lower legs are strong, there are no pubic hairs around her vagina, her vaginal mucus is wet like a wet ditch, the best age is from twenty five to thirty years old without previous birth. When she has copulation, her vagina is lubricant with her mucus, she would rock her body, her body will be covered with sweats, and she is willing to accept the manipulation of a man. If a man can have such a kind of woman, even if he does not follow the guidelines for a couple, his body still won't be hurt during copulation."

Chapter 10 Taboos for copulation

When a couple have copulation, they should observe the following taboos. They should not have copulation at the following days or time: In the first and last days of every lunar month; in the seventh and eighth and and twenty-second and twenty-third says in every lunar month; in overcast days; during solar or lunar eclipse days, earthquake, thunderstorm, extremely hot or cold days; during the days for seasonal changes from spring to summer, summer to fall, fall to winter and winter to spring; five days within praying. If the year is one's animal year, then one has to follow extra taboos, including no copulation Bing Zi and Ding Chou days after summer solstice day, Geng Shen and Xin You days after winter solstice(* all these four days are not fixed depending upon the year), immediately after washing one's head, returning from a long trip, feeling extremely tired, during extreme happiness and anger."

Pure Woman said:" Sixteenth of Lunar May is the day for copulation between the inborn vitality of sky and the earth, a couple should avoid to have copulation in the day. Otherwise they will meet their deaths within three years. How could one get to know that? One just takes a piece of new cloth and hangs the cloth at the east wall in the evening, in next day one will definitely find the cloth is stained with red. Thus a couple must follow the taboo."

CHAPTER 11 COPULATION with a ghost (wet dream)

Profound Woman asked:"Why man will have copulation with a ghost?"

Ancestor Peng said:" Because the man could not find a normal way to have copulation, thus his accumulated sexual desire could not be released, which will lead to copulation with a ghost in one's dream. In the copulation with a ghost, the man gets his pleasure like from a woman. If a man has wet dream, it means the man is possessed by ghost, because of taboo and shame, the man will not tell the truth to other people, and he is extremely satisfied with the copulation, thus a man might die due to the copulation and other people might not be able to find the real cause of his death. In order to get rid of the illness, just let the man copulate with a woman without ejaculation. They could copulate for whole night without stopping, then the man will be cured within seven days. If the patient is tired and could not do copulation, then just let his penis insert into her vagina without any movement, which could also achieve good result. If a man is with the illness without getting treatment, the man will die within several years. If one wants to prove whether such a kind of thing exists, one could go into high mountains in spring or fall, one just stays in a place between the high mountain and the deep lake, does nothing other than looking faraway and focusing his attention just for the details about copulation. Then within three days and nights, the man will definitely feel cold and hot in his body, anxious with bad mood, and dizzy with blurred eyesight. Then if the person is a man, a woman ghost will come to do copulation with him; if the person is a woman, a man ghost will come to do copulation with her, the person will get much pleasures from the copulation than with a person. If a person gets deeply involved in the process, his mind will be controlled by worry and resentment, he is controlled by evil spirit. If one comes across such a kind of patient, and the patient is a virgin or noble woman, thus one could not let another man to have copulation with her, then she could only fumigate her private part with sulfur, at the same time she should take a spoonful antler powder, she will be cured in a short while. When she is cured, one could definitely see the crying lechery ghost leaves from her place. Another method is just take the antler powder, three times per day, each time a spoonful, when the disease is cured, then she could stop taking the powder."

CHAPTER 12 HERBS TO improve sexual function

Profound Woman said:" You have already given me enough principles about copulation, I want to know do you have herbal recipes which could improve sexual function?"

Ancestor Peng said:" If one wants to have a strong healthy body, delay aging process and have sex without harming one's body, the best medicine is pilose antler. The recipe is to powder 150 grams pilose antler, then adds one each of star anise seed and monkshood to enhance the effect after making them to powder, mixes them well, each time takes one spoonful(* about 3-5 grams), three times per day, which will definitely help. Also one could boil pilose antler and wait till the water turns into yellowish, then drink the soup, it will delay the aging process. But the soup does not work as quickly as with monkshood. For the powder, it will take about twenty days to show desirable effect. One could also take Poria Cocos powder produced in west part of the country, one spoonful each time, three times per day, which will also improve sexual function and delay aging process and let the man be energetic during copulation."

Chapter 13 About sexual desire

Yellow Emperor asked a question, Pure Woman answered: " For a woman between twenty three to twenty nine, she has a strong sexual desire, always thinks about to have sex with a man, does not think about and want to have her food, even her tendon and veins show some kind of expression, her vaginal secretions will soil her shorts. It seems that the woman has a horse tail like worms about five millimeters in length in her vagina, the ones with red head will cause depression and anxiety, the ones with black head will increase her vaginal secretions. It could be cured by following method: Make a penis-like thing with flour, the length and width depends upon the vaginal size of the woman, dip the penis into a sauce, then wrap the penis with cloth, then insert the penis into her vagina to lure the worms out of her vagina. The woman could insert and withdraw the penis back and forth with stopping, as if she encounters a good doctor. Then the worms will come out of her vagina. At most sometimes more than thirty worms will come out her vagina and at least for about twenty worms."

End

Brief description about Lectures from Female Experts by the translator

Sex Bible was with one thousand three hundred sixty words in original document about principle, psychology, physiology, postures, strengthening eight body functions and getting rid of seven dysfunctions for sex etc. written in a period between 770-221BC, which is still in wide use at the moment. Chinese think food and sex are essential for the existence of human being, which might be true in other cultures too. Food is essential for the survival of an individual and sex is essential for the existence of human species. The book talks about the gist for sex of a couple is to have many times as they like, but for the man he should ejaculate as few as possible according to the age and body strength to save his vitality and energy, and for the woman she could reach her climax each time without harming her body. During copulation, man has to follow eight precepts and woman nine commandments. There are five signs, five desires and ten movements to observe, and If one sees the phenomena, then one will know the woman gets the pleasure from the copulation. Only when man has four ready statuses, then the man could do copulation. Only when woman has nine thorough functions, then the woman could do copulation. The book describes nine sex positions including Dragon Plough, Tiger Crouch, Ape Fight, Cicada Attach, Tortoise Mount, Phoenix Flight, Rabbit Suck, Fish Scale and Crane Neck, ten benefits for no ejaculation, eight ways to strengthen sexual function and seven ways to correct sexual dysfunctions such as lack of sexual desire, premature ejaculation, impotence and wet dream, making dildo, and enhancing one's sexual function and delaying aging process through Chinese medicines etc. The book covers about parts of Chinese philosophy, medicine and calendars etc., which are related to sex. Of course in the end one has to utilize what one thinks are appropriate and discards what one thinks are inappropriate as the book was written thousands years ago, this is a principle to follow for everything about learning from Confucianism.

A brief introduction of Chinese characters, philosophy, medicine and calendar by the translator

China has a continual history among the so-called four ancient civilizations. The main link for the continuity is the Chinese characters which have been created and modified continuously. The main characters, which are called complex Chinese characters and still used in Hong Kong and Taiwan, was developed around the end of Han Dynasty (8 AD), people still could read and understand materials written more than two thousand years ago; if one gets appropriate training, then one could read and understand materials about three thousand years ago(770—221 BC) in another kind of scripts which are harder to write; for some expert, they could read and understand materials about four thousand years ago (1600-771 BC) in oracle bone scripts. In 1956 after the foundation of People's Republic of China in order to promote education and reduce adult illiterates, a simplified form of Chinese characters was introduced and has been used in mainland of China. Most of educated people still could read and understand complex Chinese characters in mainland of China. With the continuity of Chinese characters, the Chinese philosophy, culture and customs could be maintained and upheld without any interruption.

Before paper was developed, one must write on wood or bamboo slips, thus one had to use as few words as possible without punctuation marks(which were introduced in Tang Dynasty around 700 AD in China). Various experts would try to understand and annotate the original document, which produced various explanations for same document. Since a long time ago, every awhile, various experts would try to annotate same document inherited from previous time or dynasties. After writing paper was introduced West Han Dynasty(202-8 BC), considerable words were added to help to define the meaning of a document, but according to current standard, there were still far fewer words. Thus annotation is still continuing. In the process for every document there would be well-recognized annotations in the period or late period.

China was an agricultural society until recently. In an agricultural society the basic unit was family, and a village was formed from families with same last family name, which means they came from same ancestor. In a family there is a hierarchy based on the authority of father. Many families with same last name would form a large family or a clan with an authoritative chief. In a family harmony is the most important thing to ensure the success of the crop fields and the family. Thus there was a saying from Confucians: if one manages a family well, then one is able to manage a state; if one manages a state well, then one is able to manage a country (the united states).

Chinese philosophy has developed with the emphasis of agriculture as its core, which is different with the industrial society. In agriculture one has to be patient and follow the seasonal changes to plant, grow, harvest and hoard, in contrast in industrial society things could be produced twenty four hours a day and years around. Five elements for material are wood, fire, soil, metal and water in Chinese philosophy. There are very complicated relationships among the elements, and depending upon the relative positions between each other, each element will produce or promote, and hinder or destroy other element, such as wood will produce fire, fire for soil, soil for metal, metal for water and water for wood, i.e. every previous element will produce or promote the one immediately followed, and the elements form a closed cycle; wood will destroy or hinder soil, fire for metal, soil for water, metal for wood, and water for soil, i.e., every element will destroy or hinder every other element followed. Chinese philosophy also holds a very important concept that every beneficial thing contains something which could destroy itself, and every bad thing contains something which could produce new self.

Chinese people prefers dynamic philosophy, when one is young, one believes in Confucius to serve people and country through one's effort and work; when one is in middle age, one believes in Taoism to retreat from worldly affairs to give space to younger generation after one achieves one's aim; when one is in old age just like a setting sun which would soon disappear behind mountains, one would believes Buddhism, the worldly thing means nothing, nothing means worldly things, till the end of the journey, nothing is more beautiful and meaningful than without being worrying and fearing. For one's whole life, only through the Confucius, Taoism and Buddhism, through serving the world, retreating from the world, and leaving the world, one's life would become a perfect harmony. Harmony is an essential concept for Chinese, one has to be in harmony with one self, family members, neighbors and nature.

Five cardinal virtues are benevolence, justice, propriety, wisdom, and honour, which are held as essential virtues gentleman should practise by Confucians. The five cardinal virtues and four seasons could also be described with the five elements, wood for benevolence and spring, fire for propriety and summer, metal for justice and autumn, water for honour and winter, soil for wisdom and all seasons. Besides Confucianism, Taoism, Buddhism and superstitions have considerable influence on Chinese people too. Taoism maintains to understand the mechanism of development of a thing, then follow its natural course with a little interference, and proposes the rulers should affect their subjects as least as possible. Buddhism maintains karma, what one gets is from what one did before and what one will get is from what one is doing. For many superstitious behaviors, which could not reasonably explained by the three thoughts, but people still follow strictly in their daily living, such as Chinese strongly believe the burial site of their ancestors including his parents has strong influence for his own and his descendants' well being, and only at certain date of lunar calendar one could get married or buried into ground etc. Right now some grave robbers for ancient graves to get antiques still depend on geomancy to find the burial site, and the geomancy is a very complicated system deriving from Chinese philosophy, calendar and geography. Chinese culture and customs are defined by these thoughts.

Chinese has a unique method to define year through combinations of ten sequential numbers from heaven branch and twelve sequential numbers from earth branch. Through such a kind of combination, every year will have an exact number, the combinations for year cycle again every sixty years due to the combinations of the numbers. Date could be defined in same way, the combinations for date cycle again every sixty days. The twelve sequential numbers from earth branch are used to define time for each day, each number represents two hours. A new day begins from Zi period, that is from 11 pm to 1 am. The first crowing of rooster happens between 1-3am, usually before 3 am. The twelve sequential numbers from earth branch could also be used to define each month for each year. A new year begins from Zi month, that is November before the period from 156-87 BC of Han Dynasty, then after from January of lunar calendar. Even with same animal year, there are still five elements to define them as the calendar for year repeat every sixty years, and only twelve animals to express birth years, thus the twelve animals will repeat five times before the calendar for year cycle again, that is depending upon the year, a snake year could be described as wood, fire, soil, metal or water snake.

Yellow Emperor is a historical figure in China. He left several classics including *Medicine* and *Chinese Sex Bible*, both are still in wide use in China. For the *Medicine*, there are two parts: first is about medicine for diagnosis and treatment, second is about Meridians and acupuncture, the *Medicine* is still used as a textbook for medical students of Traditional Chinese Medicine in university. *Chinese Sex Bible* had three women as experts: Pure Woman, Profound Woman, and Virtuoso Woman.

Based on the contents of *Chinese Sex Bible*, in early period before Song Dynasty (from 960-1279 AD) Chinese held an open mind about sex, which focuses on mutual pleasures for the couple during sex. Only in Song Dynasty two great philosophers Yi

Cheng (1033-1107 AD) and Xi Zhu (1130-1200 AD) proposed Three Essentials and Five Cardinal Virtues which were adopted by the rulers, then the focus of sex for the couple switched to the pleasure of the man. The Three Essentials are ministers must be subservient to emperor, sons must be subservient to father, and wife must be subservient to husband; Five Cardinal Virtues are benevolence, justice, propriety, wisdom, and honour. As Three Essentials and Five Cardinal Virtues were helpful for the rulers to reign country, they were followed strictly till the demise of Qing Dynasty (in 1912 AD).

Chinese has always taken a human as a whole in its medicine, which is different with western medicine specialized in different parts of human body. In Chinese medicine headache could be caused by diseases related to other parts of body such as foot, which is also a philosophical concept of Chinese that is pulling one hair will cause a cascade reaction of whole body, i.e., tiny change will lead to big impact in other unexpected parts.

Chinese holds a concept that semen is critical to one's health, and there is a saying that one drop of semen equals about ten drops of blood. Chinese still holds that a couple could benefit a lot through sex. It is still very popular in novels and online novels that a man could acquire tremendous power through sex, in the process, depending on the intention of the man, his partner could become either stronger or weaker, and vice versa. The willingness of a couple to have sex is essential for success of sex. If either of them is not willing to have sex, then forced sex will only lead to disgust.

In Traditional Chinese Medicine, the body goes from skin, muscle, tendon, bone to marrow the deepest. There are two kinds of vitality: inborn vitality and acquired vitality. Inborn vitality comes from one's parents and during pregnancy. Acquired vitality comes from food, exercise etc. There is a very important concept of the balance between Ying (negative) and Yang (positive). Such as in this book, fire (positive) is used to indicate a man, and water (negative) is used to indicate a woman, thus for sex they have to maintain balance to benefit from the process.

In Traditional Chinese Medicine, a human has heart, liver, spleen, lung and kidney as five organs, small intestine, gall bladder, stomach, bladder, large intestine and three Jiaos as six viscera, the organs have a Ying quality and viscera have a Yang quality, each organ has a corresponding one of the five elements such as wood for liver, fire for heart, soil for spleen, metal for lung and water for kidney, thus the organs also have the producing or promoting, and destroying or hindering functions like the five elements. The one of organs forms a pair with one of viscera to help each other, thus liver for gallbladder, heart for small intestine, spleen for stomach, lung for large intestine and kidney for bladder. Three Jiaos are quite unique concepts, they include upper, middle and lower Jiaos. For Upper Jiao, it means everything in chest above septum including heart and lung; for Middle Jiao, it means everything in abdomen below the septum and above the umbilicus including spleen, stomach, liver and gall bladder; for Lower Jiao it means everything in abdomen below the umbilicus including kidney, small and large intestine, bladder and uterus. Three Jiaos could be taken as three integrated parts which Traditional Chinese Medicine think necessary to get understanding, diagnosis and treatment of various diseases.

In Traditional Chinese Medicine, there are three essential concepts: Vitality, Body Fluid and Blood. Vitality moves blood and body fluid around, body fluid is the liquid out of the blood vessel, blood and body fluid nurture the body and its vitality.

Chinese people still have a strong belief in Traditional Chinese Medicine, particularly for chronic illness such tiredness, chronic gastric illness etc. and some acute illness such as colds. Before the western medicine was introduced into China, Chinese people depended upon Traditional Chinese Medicine for everything including acute illness and bone fracture etc. Many Chinese people still prefers to go to Traditional Chinese Medicine doctor for dislocation or bone fracture today. Tuo Hua was a famous doctor (145-208 AD) who developed anesthesia for surgery, and it was said at that time he could open skull to do operation. Many famous people in Chinese history lived for more than seventy or eighty years old due to practice of Chinese philosophy, culture and medicine. In a word, in China everything is connected with other things, everything has two sides, none could only get benefit without getting harm in the process, thus one has to maintain balance and harmony.

Did you love *Sex Bible*? Then you should read *Gem & Geson: Meet Again*[1] by Sweet One!

[2]

A love story between two men from two well-known families engaged in tea business. Shrewdning Wong, the influential female manager of tea business of the Fangs, sets fire to the mansion and kills the parents of Geson Fang. As a result, Geson becomes the crippled puppet head of the Fang family, and he is determined to fight back and awaits an opportunity. He, however, has to cut himself off Gem Fore for whom he has had affections since his childhood because he does not want to get his sweetheart involved with his revenge. Gem becomes the

---

1. https://books2read.com/u/meqD2Z

2. https://books2read.com/u/meqD2Z

substitute for the bride, who should have been his younger sister in an arranged marriage, and marries Geson. Since then their love has grown deeper and deeper. Moreover, Gem assists Geson in bringing Shrewdning Wong down. At last the couple have a happy ending.